TRAP KITCHEN

BANGIN' RECIPES FROM COMPTON

Vodka & Milk

Trap Kitchen ©2017 by Malachi Jenkins, Roberto Smith & Marisa Mendez
Printed in the United States of America

First Edition:

Book Design: PiXiLL Designs

Cataloging in Publication data is on file with the library of Congress

ISBN 9780997146264 (trade paperback)

TABLE OF CONTENTS

INTRODUCTION

If you're reading this cookbook, you should already know who we are. I'm Spank, my business partner is News, and we are motherfucking Trap Kitchen. Making a cookbook was only right at this point. We got shit jumping on social media with our plates, we got everyone from the big homie Snoop Dogg to Kendrick Lamar to Wiz Khalifa to Justin Bieber requesting our catering, we got merchandise, and now we got our own book. We could have gone all corporate and shit and made this sound hella prim and proper, but we ain't selling out like that. We ain't switched up since day one, and we ain't about to start now!

But on a serious note, we want to inspire more unconventional chefs. The people that are artistic in the kitchen; we want them to put a twist on our recipes with their own creativity. That's what Trap Kitchen is all about! Lord knows we didn't come from conventional backgrounds, but we avoided being another statistic and actually did something we're proud of.

And everybody got a story, right? We have one too. Like I said, it wasn't the most conventional route, but I wouldn't change it. We're here now, cuz. It's on.

STARTED FROM THE BOTTOM

The first thing I ever cooked was motherfucking eggs and pancakes. It wasn't no special moment really, but I was like 7-years-old and my mom was up cooking for my friends that had slept over and I wanted to help.

As a kid, you want some type of maturity; something to be respected for. I was the youngest in the house and the only boy, and that day, my mom let me be a part of something. Who knew that two decades and a ton of dumb shit later, it would be what puts the blue and red shit to the side to change my life, News' life and our people's' lives too.

After that day in the kitchen, I started fucking around with little shit here and there. When I went to summer camp that summer, you got to pick a little job, so I picked the kitchen so I could eat first and get the leftovers too. That shit was fire. Then, when I was in the Boy Scouts, it was like same shit. When we went to camp, I was in the Boy Scouts, it was like same shit. When we went to camp, I was designated camp cook to help one of the Scout Masters cook, you feel me? Just like with my moms, it was was just a sense of maturity to it. It was like damn, cuz - I got a duty!

Spaghetti was like my first big meal I made for everybody in the Scouts. I was like 11, and I did that shit on an outside stove. Niggas was really feeling it, so I started to think like, maybe I'm kind of nice with this. I'm starting to come home and ask my mom if can I cook this, can I help you cook that, feel me? By the time I'm in middle school, she was working at night, my sisters would be out and my pops – I never knew that nigga - so I would be in the crib just cooking some easy shit. I'd keep it light with easy shit like tacos, so I wouldn't burn myself or fuck something up. I wish I could give y'all some fairy tale ending like this shit kept me out of trouble as I got older, but I'd be lying my ass off.

BEAT THE CASE BOYZ

I started getting in trouble in high school, but it wasn't nothing crazy. I never went to juvie or nothing like that, but when I finally did catch a case, it went from 0 to 100 REAL fucking quick. The crazy shit was – I didn't even do it! It was a mistaken identity, and I went through hell for it. I was a senior in high school, and I was facing life without the chance of parole.

I went to Compton High, and the courthouse was right next to my school. I'd be walking past the homies while they going to lunch, and I'm going to fight for my life for some wild shit that I ain't even do. I'll tell you what, though – I was the first nigga to hit county! All the homies and had to camp and shit, but that's not real jail. I was in with the big boys.

The details of the whole case ain't really necessary, but just know it was some real shit. It's hard enough trying to fucking graduate; imagine doing that while fighting a case that would ruin your entire life. Then there's the money too. You're 18 and trying to save up for prom and grad parties and all that shit, and now I'm adding lawyer fees and 10% of my $100,000 bond to it. My mother made it happen, though. She spent like $50,000 on me, man; put our house up and everything. The person who wrongfully accused me ended up apologizing later, like, "I'm sorry; my family put me up to it! I just chose any story!" Life is crazy.

I went to jail two more times that year for dumb shit – all while I'm in the middle of my trial for the first case. I beat every case, though. I had a bomb ass lawyer and I don't know where I would be now without her.

THE NEXT LEVEL

With all that shit behind me, I knew I needed to do something productive. I went to community college, I got a job and I was trying to do music. Usually in the hood, you either trying to become a ball player or a rapper/producer, and my story wasn't no different. I don't know too many homies who were trying to be a big time chef, but I hope there are kids seeing now that that's an option.

Mind you, I was always still cooking, you feel me? It wasn't in the sense that I thought I was gonna be cooking before, but I needed to eat. I was still gang-banging hard too, because that whole trial had me on edge and a nigga stayed on edge.

When my mom got transferred to Washington D.C. a few years later, she left me the crib in Compton, and it was ON. My crib damn near became a frat house. We were having hella parties, and I would cook for every one of them and charge $10 to get in. To be real, that shit was on some unity shit even back then, because all hoods – enemy or not – was coming to the crib.

The HOA used to have meetings about my house because of all the noise and the traffic. They even got to the sheriff station in City Hall and threw a fucking block party in front of my house, with MY address on the flyer. They were trying to make a statement, and I wasn't backing down because no one ever addressed me properly. It eventually got to my mom though because we ended up in the newspaper and one of her friends told her, so we had to make some changes. By then, I was tired of living there anyway because the roommate I'd had kept letting anybody in the crib at any time of day – and the commercial I saw for Le Cordon Bleu College of Culinary Arts Las Vegas couldn't have come at a better time.

BRIGHT LIGHTS, BIG CITY

At this point, I was working two jobs, hustling shit on the side and producing music, and I wanted to get away. The Le Cordon commercial was the answer to everything – I can get into cooking professionally, and I can get away to Vegas. So I just went. I shut the house down, moved to Vegas and just made a way for myself out there. I'd still get into some dumb shit here and there, but I would make it to class every Monday! That changed quick when my little homie came to visit and ended up getting smoked right in front of me.

I tried to save his life, but as I took him to the hospital, he died in the car. That shit will fuck anybody up. I had to take some time off of school (which they allowed,) but when I came back just a few months later, they'd changed up the entire program! I'd come in as a savory chef, and it was supposed to be a two-year program to get your Associate of Arts. They switched that shit to basically a nine-month cooking course with a certificate, and I said fuck that. I had clientele in Vegas by this time, though. Pimps, hoes, rappers, dealers; everyone was buying plates off of me, because word of mouth kept spreading that I cheffed it up. But I wanted to be home in L.A. My family was looking at me funny because I wasn't going to school anymore, and it wasn't no real job opportunities out in Vegas. I'm like fuck this shit; I'm about to go back to the hood where I know I could make some real money, so I moved back.

When I was back in L.A., I had a plan to go to the Art Institute because they had a BA for culinary school. I enrolled, but I didn't do that shit either. Right before I started, I ended up getting brutally beat up by the police after a high-speed chase; I'm talking beat to a fucking pulp. It was another fucked up situation, and they ended up dropping every charge and just gave me resisting arrest.

At this point, I had been staying with my aunt and uncle, and they wasn't fucking with the shit I was getting into so they didn't want me staying with them anymore. Now I'm homeless and just wandering from living in my car, to staying with my homies, different girls – it was a weird period. I went back to Vegas for a little bit because I knew I had a place to stay there, and I ended up meeting these guys from Portland who fucked with my cooking so heavy, they flew me back out to Portland with them to cook for their events and different shit. Finally, shit started making sense. I was making good money, I was stable, my mom was happy because I wasn't getting in trouble anymore and I was doing good.

For about three years, I bounced around between Portland, L.A. and Vegas. I was hustling a ton of other shit too, just trying to make every dollar I could. A friend introduced me to News around this time, and we both clicked because we had that hustler mentality. He was an even bigger hustler than me, and we were out here getting money together for a minute. The problem was – he kept going in and out of jail! It was only county, but it was slowing him up. My work started to slow down too, and at one point, we met up like, 'What the fuck are we gonna do?' He had this idea like, 'Fuck it, let's sell some food!' He noticed how people would always comment on my pictures of food on Instagram, asking where they could buy it, and he saw an opportunity there. That's where Trap Kitchen was born.

THE REAL TRAP KITCHEN

We started off small, just helping my boy Taco Mel out. He was another chef from around our way. I was also promoting parties on the side as another hustle, but once I fell out with the person I was promoting with, I decided to put my all into my cooking shit. News wasn't as big on cooking as I was, but I showed him the ropes and he picked that shit up quick.

We used to go half with Taco Mel and have Taco Tuesdays in the backyard and it was just crazy. We had this whole new wave of shit! Then me and News started selling breakfast just on Instagram, and we'd sell out so quick. That's what we built our platform off of. And just like that, every week it would get bigger. Every month, we started hearing from bigger names that wanted us to cater their function. Being from around the way, people like Snoop and Kendrick have been tapped in with us for a while, so they really looked out with giving us opportunities to get our name out there. In just a few years, we've grown from two guys coming together to figure out the next hustle, to having a full brand and business. We out here, cuz!

That being said, welcome to the Trap. You'll find recipes for signature staples of many meals, and it will have you set for your family function, your backyard cookout, or just trying to impress whoever you got coming over tonight. This is only volume one, by the way. You ain't getting rid of us for a LONG time!

GRAVY

Gravy is really a marriage between the meat and the carbs, whether it be pasta, noodles or rice or whatever. Some type of gravy needs to go in a hearty meal! It's part of comfort food. It's like damn, this is slapping when it's cold outside and you got this warm gravy. My mama used to make gravy every Thanksgiving, and that was always my favorite. It's so simple and it does so much for the plate. It's just bomb, cuz.

IT'S GRAVY, BABY

(Apple Gravy)

Dice up the onions, garlic, apples, turkey neck. Sauté them up in a pan with oil and butter, and add your flour as you're doing so. Keep stirring until it makes a roux and gets thick. Don't let the flour burn! You want it to be blonde-colored. When the onions and the apples start to caramelize, then you add your chicken broth. Bring it to a boil, and keep stirring until it gets thick. Then let it simmer for about 35 minutes. You can add cinnamon and/or a little bit of allspice if you want, but it's optional.

IT'S GRAVY, BABY

- Minced garlic
- Diced onions
- ½ cup oil
- ½ cup flour
- 1 cup sliced green apples
- 2 cups chicken broth
- Kosher salt
- Black pepper
- 2 tablespoons butter
- 1 smoked turkey neck
- Cinnamon (optional)
- Allspice (optional)

WHOSE CRANS IS THIS?

(Cranberry Gravy)

Dice up the onions and garlic, add your cranberries and sauté them in pan with oil and butter, and add your flour as you're doing so. Bring to a boil, keep stirring until it thickens. When the onions start to caramelize, add the beef broth or beef stock. Cook for 20 minutes until the flour taste is out. Keep stirring it and if it reduces, keep stirring and add a little bit of water. Let simmer for about 35 minutes.

WHOSE CRANS IS THIS?

- Minced garlic
- Diced onions
- ½ cup oil
- ½ cup flour
- ½ cup of cranberries
- 2 cups of beef broth or beef stock
- Kosher salt
- Black pepper
- 2 tablespoons butter

SIDES

I REALLY BEAN IT
(Green Beans with Turkey Tails and Potatoes)

If you prefer canned or fresh green beans, it's up to you. Get a sauté pan or pot - whichever you prefer to cook the green beans in. You can use olive oil or vegetable oil just to coat the pan. Dice up the bell peppers, the onions and the turkey tails.

Make sure the green beans are snapped and clean. Some people leave the ends on, some people don't. It don't really matter what you do. Cook it to your preference. Personally, we like to cook them until they damn near bust open. But for this, you can use French cut and you won't even have to trip. Set those to the side.

For those that don't mind pork on their fork, you can add bacon grease here too. You damn near don't even gotta use no seasonings when you put that shit in there. It be so bomb! Even though we're cooking turkey, we got bacon grease in there! But it's optional. That's all on you, bruh.

As you're sautéing the ingredients, add the seasoning in bit by bit. Sauté them until the turkey tails start turning soft. Continue to season them as they get softer. Then you add your chicken broth in there, put a top over it and let it come to a boil. Then you throw in your green beans and your diced potatoes.

You can use golden potatoes or you can use baby red potatoes. You can cook those for like 45 minutes on medium heat. Bring them to a boil and you let them simmer. Then add it all together and it's good!

I REALLY BEAN IT

- Minced garlic
- 1 onion
- 1 qt of chicken broth
  (with 2 cups of water)
- Garlic powder
- Onion powder
- Seasoning salt
- Pepper
- Cajun seasoning
- 2 habanero peppers
- ½ bottle of habanero pepper sauce
- 2 smoked turkey necks
- 2 bags of fresh picked greens

COLLARD IF YA HEAR ME

(Collard Greens with Turkey Necks)

Get a sauté pan and coat with olive oil or vegetable oil. Dice up the habanero pepper, the onions and the turkey necks.

Take your greens and clean them and cut the stems. Some people like stems so keep them if you want, but it's really up to you. Sauté your greens with the mix you diced up, adding the pepper sauce, Cajun seasoning, onion powder, seasoning salt, pepper, minced garlic and garlic powder as you sauté. Then you add the chicken broth, and these got to cook for like, 2 hours.

COLLARD IF YA HEAR ME

- Minced garlic
- 1 onion
- 1 qt of chicken broth
  (with 2 cups of water)
- Garlic powder
- Onion powder
- Seasoning salt
- Pepper
- Cajun seasoning
- 2 habanero peppers
- ½ bottle of habanero pepper sauce
- 2 smoked turkey necks
- 2 bags of fresh picked greens

BYRD GANG
(Chicken Rice)

Take two cups of rice and boil them in cold water. Once they come to a boil, add your chicken bouillon to it. Leave them simmering for a bit.

Dice up your green bell peppers, and in a separate pan, take the bell peppers, the ground chicken or sausage and your minced garlic and brown it. Season to your liking with salt, pepper and Cajun seasoning. Then add it to your rice and bring it back to a boil. Then let it simmer for 15-20 minutes until the rice is cooked through.

BYRD GANG

- 2 cups long grain rice
- 1 chicken bouillon cube or powder
- ½ pound of spicy ground chicken sausage
  (or ground chicken)
- 1 green bell pepper
- Minced garlic
- Salt
- Pepper
- Cajun seasoning

WHAT'S THE YAMS?
(Candied Yams)

This gon' bust down.

Peel the yams, cut them to your liking, We be cutting them into thin medallions (circular - like a quarter inch thick.) Boil them until they get soft, which is usually for one hour.

Take your butter - you can melt the sticks yourself in the microwave or just throw them in whole. Put hella brown sugar - over a cup. Go crazy with hella cinnamon - you have to taste it. Maybe it's 2 tablespoons, maybe it's 3. Add a cup of orange juice. Top it with a cup of regular sugar.

In a baking pan, set it in the oven uncovered for 1 hour. For the last 2 minutes, top it with marshmallows and put back in until the marshmallows turn light brown. You don't want to burn your shit!

WHAT'S THE YAMS?

- 2 lbs of yams
- 1 cup of brown sugar (minimum)
- 1 bag of marshmallows
- 2 sticks of butter
- 1 cup of orange juice
- 2-3 tablespoons cinnamon
- 1 cup of cane sugar

YOU WERE MY CINNAMON APPLE!

(Apple Cinnamon Corn Bread)

Follow the instructions on the cornbread box from your local store. It's not that hard, cuz. We're not grinding up cornmeal out here. We're not finna bore y'all! You want to get this in the oven now, because you know the kids is on you!

Dice up the apples. In a small pan, sauté your apples and butter and sugar until they're caramelized. Add that to your cornbread mix after your mix your cornbread in. Mix it in good.

Bake it in a muffin pan for about 15 minutes at 375 degrees, until it's nice and toasted.

YOU WERE MY CINNAMON APPLE!

- 2 tablespoons of sugar
- ½ stick of butter (melted)
- 2 teaspoons of cinnamon
- Cornbread mix
- ⅓ cup milk
- 1 egg
- ¼ to ⅓ cup sour cream
- 1 tablespoon honey
- 1 cup of diced green apples

TRAP MAC

(4 Cheese Mac & Cheese)

We got the best mac and cheese in Los Angeles. We stand by that.

Boil the noodles until they're well done. Like, blow the noodles up, cuz. Don't cook them to Al dente. Almost overcook them but don't. Strain them of course. Put them back in the pot. Season the noodles with half a stick of butter to coat them, add onion powder, seasoning salt, lots of pepper - this is the main thing about mac and cheese. It's the balance to the richness of the cheese so the more pepper, the better. Add your dried parsley flakes and two dollops of sour cream. Add your mushroom soup, then your cheddar cheese soup.

Add your cheese grated and shredded, and mix until you hear that gooey noise like you in some guts. Add your carnation milk and cheese whiz and all that shit in together. Take a baking pan or sheet, spread the mix in, make it even in the pan and shred up the rest of the cheese blend and top it.

Make sure all the edges is covered! There's no holes. You don't want to see NO noodles; that's how thick your top has to be. Once you topped it with the cheese, top it with some pepper and parsley. Bake on 425 degrees until the edges start browning and crusting. It's fucking nuts, cuz! Once you break through the surface of that shit, it's so gooey and cheesy! Damn!

TRAP MAC

- 1 box of small macaroni noodles
- ½ lb sharp cheddar cheese
- ½ lb Kobe jack cheddar cheese
- ½ lb Monterey jack cheese
- ½ lb Mild cheddar cheese
- 2 cans Campbell's cheddar cheese soup
- 2 cans Campbell's roasted garlic mushroom soup
- 1 can Carnation evaporated milk
- ½ cup Kraft cheese whiz in a jar
  (It's hard to find but you need to find it!)
- Dried parsley flakes
- Cajun seasoning
- Hella pepper
- Seasoning salt
- ½ stick of butter
- 2 dollops sour cream

BACON AND YOUNG CHEESY

(Bacon Mac)

Add real bacon bits or fry up fully cooked and chopped up thick-cut applewood bacon. You can add as much as you want. Who doesn't love bacon? But, ONLY use as a topping!

BACON AND YOUNG CHEESY

- All ingredients in the Trap Mac
- Bacon bits

ASPARAGUS $PEARS

(Asparagus)

Sauté in a pan with olive oil and season as you go for 3 to 4 minutes, then put a lid on for the last minute. Them motherfuckers don't take no time.

ASPARAGUS $PEARS

- Lemon pepper
- Tony's Cajun seasoning
- Vegetable or olive oil
- Asparagus

POP POP POTATO SALAD

Quarter your potatoes, boil them until soft which is like 15 to 20 minutes; maybe 30 at the most. Drain the potatoes.

Take your relish, throw it in a bowl with mayo, mustard, sugar, pepper, seasoning salt and paprika, and mix it together until it becomes a creamy consistency. Then add your eggs chopped up. To be festive, you can cut them in half and make an egg salad and put it back in there. Potato salad be on hit, though.

POP POP POTATO SALAD

- 4 lbs of red potatoes
- ½ cup relish
- ½ cup mayonnaise
- ½ cup mustard
- 2 tablespoons sugar
- 4 tablespoons pepper
- 4 tablespoons seasoning salt
- 1 tablespoon paprika
- Boiled eggs

RUSTIC POTATO SALAD

Take the diced vegetables and minced garlic in a pan with oil and sauté until soft, then add the potatoes in. This is all in grease, as there's no water needed! Sauté until potatoes get soft.

Crack 5 eggs and season with salt, pepper and milk, and whip until fluffy. Once your potatoes are cooked and soft, then add the eggs and scramble until they're fluffy and yellow. Add bacon bits and chopped sausage if you want to get crazy.

RUSTIC POTATO SALAD

- 5 eggs
- 1.5lbs baby golden potatoes
- 1 bell pepper
- ½ onion
- ¾ cup of milk
- Salt
- Pepper
- 2 tablespoons minced garlic
- Bacon bits (optional)
- Chopped sausage (optional)

'LIC ME GOOD THEN I'LL PUT THE MASH WITH THE LOBSTER

(Lobster Garlic Mashed Potatoes)

Boil the potatoes (skin on) until a fork can go right through them. That's how you test them. Drain the pot, put them back in and add butter and start mashing them. If you got a cake beater or some shit, it'll be even better in there. It'll be more fluffy and rich but if you got a cold wrist game, whip that shit up. Add in the kosher salt, white pepper, whole pint of sour cream and chives.

Take the lobster out of the shell, clean it and take the boo-boo out. In a pan with olive oil, sauté it with minced garlic in a pan and drain and add to your mashed potato mix. It's so fire, I could smell it right now. Make that with some motherfucking chicken breast or a steak. Garnish with parsley.

'LIC ME GOOD THEN I'LL PUT THE MASH WITH THE LOBSTER

- 1 bag baby golden potatoes
- 1 pint sour cream
- 1 bundle of chives
- 2 lobster tails
- 3 tablespoons minced garlic
- 1 stick butter
- Seasoning salt
- Parsley
- 1 teaspoon lemon juice

CHICKEN & TURKEY

Some of our chicken dishes are infamous. One time, Tyga asked us to cater one of his parties, and he requested our chicken wings, BBQ chicken, quesadillas, tacos and French fries. We're at the house and it's everybody from Kanye West to Kim Kardashian, The Game, Baron Davis, Scott Disick, Chris Brown, August Alsina, Post Malone, Keyshia Cole – motherfuckin' everybody was there! Kanye fucking dug his hands all in the fries and our chicken, eating like, "I gotta take this back to Kim." She was upstairs, but he really made sure she got some of our chicken too. Everybody loved the shit.

CHICKEN CURRY IN THE POT, BOY

Dice your onions, mince your garlic. Cube up the chicken strips and the potatoes. In a bowl, add seasoning salt, minced garlic powder, onions, black pepper and Jamaican curry powder to the chicken after you coat it in oil. Everybody don't like a lot, so everything here is to taste.

Cut up the scotch bonnet pepper. In a pot, sauté the ingredients in vegetable oil until they turn soft and start browning. Then add your chicken broth. Bring to a simmer, and cook until the potatoes start to thicken up like stew.

Shit, cook the rice in a small pot with 2 cups of water. We ain't gotta necessarily tell y'all how to cook the rice, because y'all should know how to cook that shit if you're already using a cookbook.

CHICKEN CURRY IN THE POT, BOY

- 4 potatoes
- 2 tablespoons of Jamaican curry powder
- Half an onion
- 2 tablespoons minced garlic
- Bottled scotch bonnet - *to taste depending on how you like it. I pour the whole bottle in there*
- 1 scotch bonnet pepper

- Pepper
- Chicken broth
- 2 lbs boneless skinless chicken tenders
- 1-2 cups of white rice
- Vegetable oil

IS THAT YOUR CHICK'N MAC?
(Chicken Mac)

Follow the instructions to Trap Mac to make the mac.

Small dice the tenders. Sauté them in the pan and add some salt and pepper to season the chicken. Once they're fully cooked through, drain them and the excess fat and oil and spread them over the surface of your mac.

IS THAT YOUR CHICK' N MAC?

- ½ lb boneless skinless chicken tenders
- 1 box of small macaroni noodles
- ½ lb sharp cheddar cheese
- ½ lb Kobe jack cheddar cheese
- ½ lb Monterey jack cheese
- ½ lb Mild cheddar cheese
- 2 cans Campbell's cheddar cheese soup
- 2 cans Campbell's roasted garlic mushroom soup
- 1 can Carnation evaporated milk
- ½ cup Kraft cheese whiz in a jar
  (It's hard to find but you need to find it!)
- Dried parsley flakes
- Cajun seasoning
- Hella pepper
- Seasoning salt
- ½ stick of butter
- 2 dollops sour cream

TOO MUCH SAUCE BBQ CHICKEN
(BBQ Chicken)

Coat the chicken with mustard lightly. Add your seasonings to taste. You can also bake them in the oven for about 30 minutes at 375 degrees, and then finish them for another 30 on the grill.

This shit is so fire that you don't need barbecue sauce, but feel free to have it on the side if you want it.

TOO MUCH SAUCE BBQ CHICKEN

- 16 pieces of chicken drumsticks and wings
- 2 tablespoons garlic powder
- 2 tablespoons onion powder
- 2 tablespoons dried rosemary
- HELLA Chef Merito Pollo seasoning
  (Even though we season our chicken with regular shit, we still use this heavy!)
- 2 tablespoons garlic salt (We would say Lawry's but do whatever you want!)
- 2 tablespoons pepper
- Mustard
- BBQ sauce (optional)

THE CHOP BOYZ WITH TURK

(Turkey Chops)

Coat the turkey chops in olive oil and add your seasonings. Grill them on a mesquite charcoal fire for 15 minutes. Take them off, put them in the pan with some chicken broth and cover them and steam them on 400 degrees for another 20 minutes, because you need that flavor.

They gonna be soft, breaking apart and moist!

THE CHOP BOYZ WITH TURK

- Kosher salt
- Coarse pepper
  (It's kind of thick but it's bomb though)
- Smoked paprika
- Onion powder
- Olive oil
- Cast iron griddle
- Turkey chops (Only certain butchers offer turkey chops. We get them from Mr. T's Meat Market on Western and 62nd, but if you're not from around the way, find them somewhere.)
- Mesquite charcoal
- ½ cup chicken broth

CHICK UP ON IT

(Chicken Chops)

Most butchers offer chicken chops at the meat market, so you'll find it in there. You can follow the same instructions for the turkey chops. We ain't finna tell y'all the same shit twice.

CHICK UP ON IT

- Kosher salt
- Coarse pepper
  (It's kind of thick but it's bomb though)
- Smoked paprika
- Onion powder
- Olive oil
- Cast iron griddle
- Chicken Chops
- Mesquite charcoal
- ½ cup chicken broth

WHAT SHE ORDER? CHICKEN BAKED?
(Savory Baked Chicken)

Coat the chicken with olive oil, and in a bowl, massage your seasonings into it. Make love to yo' meat. You gotta massage the meat! Place it on top of the baking rack in the pan, and you can break up your rosemary and spread it out throughout the chicken on the rack.

Bake them at uncovered 375 for one hour to one hour and 15 minutes. You have to flip every piece of chicken to make sure it's being cooked. You don't want it to be light-skinned.

This next step is hella unhealthy, but it tastes so good. You can base your chicken in its own grease. You keep scooping that juice up and pour it on top. But if you on your healthy shit, we wouldn't suggest this.

WHAT SHE ORDER? CHICKEN BAKED?

- 2 lbs of drumstick chicken wings
- 1 bundle of rosemary
- Olive oil
- 2 tablespoons parsley
- 2 tablespoons salt
- 2 tablespoons pepper
- 2 tablespoons minced garlic
- 2 tablespoons Chef Merito
- Pollo Seasoning
- Baking rack
- Pan

Mustard is the key! Don't ask questions!

First clean the chicken. Rinse it and all that, then take some mustard and coat it and massage it. Add your seasoning. Season your flour if you don't have dixie friend. Use pepper and seasoning salt.

Then take a grocery bag and double it up, put your flour/chicken fry in the bag. Make sure your chicken is fully coated - crevices in the wings and all. Can't miss no parts because when you fry it'll be blotches. Take about 8 pieces at a time, tie the bag up and SHAKE AND BAKE! Press your pieces in deep and make sure every corner is covered in flour and then you shake it up. Use one hand to throw the chicken in the deep fryer and one hand to take it out of the flour so you don't cross-contaminate or mess up the oil, because you'll keep dropping in it.

Make sure the oil is at least like 4 something. You want to make sure the deep fryer is at its max temperature to ensure your chicken is crispy as fuck, like the yo' outfit on the first day of school! Fry the chicken until it floats. Once it floats to the surface, it's done.

Then put it on a baking rack and keep it elevated in open air.

Follow the waffle instructions, but add cinnamon to your mix. That's what we do. Water and waffle mix and cinnamon. It's not no way to make this shit sound fancy, cuz. It's really simple. Use melted butter instead of spray - spray is healthier but butter tastes better.

You can top with fresh diced strawberry and powdered sugar if you're trying to impress somebody.

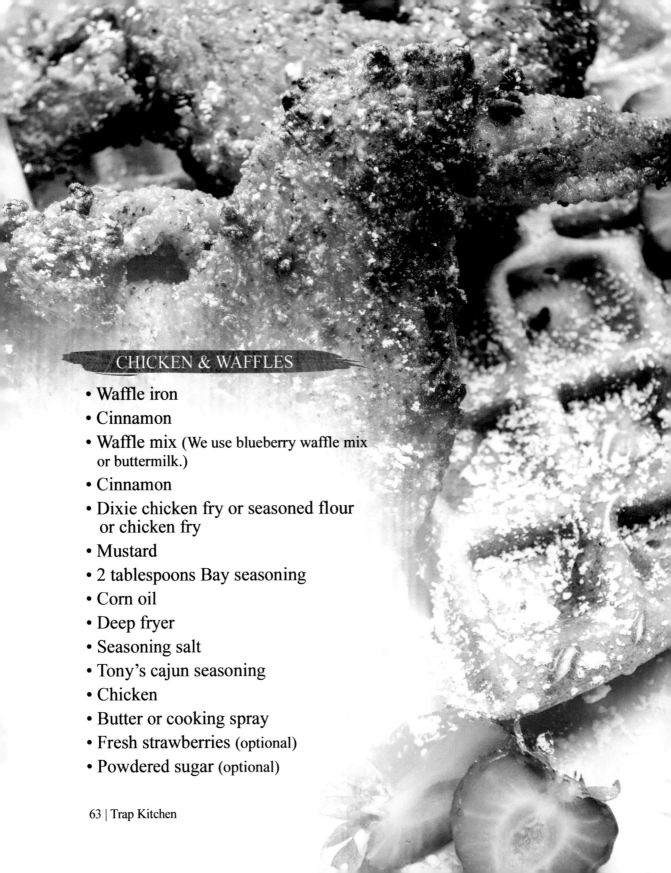

CHICKEN & WAFFLES

- Waffle iron
- Cinnamon
- Waffle mix (We use blueberry waffle mix or buttermilk.)
- Cinnamon
- Dixie chicken fry or seasoned flour or chicken fry
- Mustard
- 2 tablespoons Bay seasoning
- Corn oil
- Deep fryer
- Seasoning salt
- Tony's cajun seasoning
- Chicken
- Butter or cooking spray
- Fresh strawberries (optional)
- Powdered sugar (optional)

SEAFOOD & STEAK

One of the first meals we really perfected was our pineapple bowls, which is the first up in this category. About three years ago, we first introduced them by doing Pineapple Fridays, and it was such a hit that people were coming from out of town for them. At the time, we had a set-up in a first-floor apartment building, and people were able to actually drive up to our window and pick up their orders.

The manager of the complex was racist as fuck and hated us, and they assumed that because of the traffic, we were selling drugs. So one day, two first-time customers had traveled all the way to us from out of town for our Pineapple Bowls, and someone had actually dropped a dime on us to the police. Our customers end up getting pulled over by an unmarked car on their way out of the complex, with the cops telling them, 'Yeah, we got word that drugs are being sold over here, and we just want to search your car.'

Of course, all they found was food when they searched it. Good ass food, at that! The cops obviously had to drop the case and they told the customers to have a nice day. It's really always some crazy shit in my life!

THROW DEM BOWLS

(Pineapple Bowls)

There's hella different ways you can make this. You always start by cutting the pineapple in half from the bottom to the crown, and gutting it into a bowl. Then boil the jasmine rice and put it in the bowl, then put it to the side.

We included all of the ingredients above, but you can pick and choose which way you want to do it.

- Pineapple
- 2 cups of Jasmine rice (per bowl)
- ¼ lb of boneless skinless chicken thigh meat
  (You can use chicken breast if you don't like
  dark meat, but we use this because to us it tastes
  so much better. It's fucking bomb.)
- Bottle of Teriyaki sauce
- Sriracha
- Sweet chili sauce
- Green onions
- Sesame seeds
- ¼ lb of beef short rib
- ¼ lb of salmon
- ¼ lb of large shrimp
- ¼ lb of king crab
- 1 lobster
- Worcestershire sauce
- Kikkoman pineapple ginger marinade
- Mesquite charcoal
- Chef Merito

TRIO - CHICKEN, SALMON, SHRIMP

(Or you can do chicken and shrimp, chicken and salmon or salmon and shrimp)

LOBSTER & SHRIMP

(People be asking for that heavy!)

LOBSTER & SHORT RIB OR
CHICKEN & SHORT RIB

(This is when you trying to stunt!)

DEADLIEST CATCH
(Lobster, salmon, crab, shrimp)

VEGAN BOWL

(This would include yellow squash, red and green bell peppers, onions, zucchini, garlic or a plant-based vegan meat. Sauté in "butter" after you dice them all up.)

Sauté the shrimp in butter, sweet chili sauce, pepper, Old Bay.

Broil your salmon in the broiler with melted butter, parsley, old bay, pepper and Tony's Cajun seasoning. Broil for about 15 minutes until firm, nice and toasty. It's like it has a nice coat. The texture has to be kind of firm and crispy. Now, some people do like salmon soft and pink, and you can eat salmon raw, but we don't need y'all trying to get fancy and fucking some shit up. This is how we make our shit. We broil it.

Take a lobster and chop it in half right down the middle with the shell on. Clean it, get the boo boo out. Quarter your king crab legs so they fit in the bowl. Take a pan, put your lobster and your crab in there together with melted butter, old bay, pepper and Tony's Cajun seasoning and bake for 15 minutes.

Take your boneless chicken and your beef short ribs and season them in onion powder, seasoning salt, pepper, Worcestershire sauce, teriyaki sauce and Kikkoman, and grill over mesquite charcoal. For the chicken you use Chef Merito's pollo seasoning as well, and add more teriyaki sauce to coat it once it's fully cooked. Chop it up and put it in your bowl.

In a squeeze bottle, you use the same teriyaki marinade you cooked with and drizzle it over the rest. Then squeeze sriracha over it lightly, take chopped and diced green onions and small sesame seeds and some of the gutted pineapple and use it all as a topping.

SKRRRRRT STEAK
(Skirt Steak)

Coat the meat in the vegetable oil, Cajun seasoning, onion powder, seasoning salt, pepper and Worcestershire sauce. Heat up the griddle and cook it depending on how you like it. We like it medium rare, so we sear it on the side real quick and keep it bloody. (Don't get it fucked up though, cuz.)

Add in your tablespoon of butter while it's cooking for the last minute, and it just disperses over the steak. Let the steak rest to release all those juices. There will be juices everywhere!

SKRRRRRT STEAK

- Cast iron griddle
- Vegetable oil
- 3 lbs skirt steak
- 1 teaspoon Cajun seasoning
- 1 teaspoon onion powder
- 1 teaspoon seasoning salt
- 1 teaspoon pepper
- 1 teaspoon Worcestershire sauce
- 1 tablespoon butter

STEAK CARE

(Steak & Lobster Enchilada Pie)

Take a pan and coat it with the red enchilada sauce. Lay the tortillas flat to cover the surface of the pan - might be 2, might be 3. Spread a light layer of cheese and green onions, some more cheese, then the carne asada. Cover with more cheese and green onions, and repeat another layer of tortillas. Repeat these steps until you have 3 layers. The cheese is the glue that connects the tortillas to the meat.

Take 2 lobsters, clean them, dice them and sauté them in a pan with oil until the meat is done, and add it to your steak. Once you have at least 2 layers, take the raw diced lobster and the leftover steak (because I'm pretty sure there's gonna be some) and you sprinkle that over the top as your garnish.

Bake that for 30 minutes on 425 degrees. Boom!

STEAK CARE

- 45 count corn tortillas
- 2 cans red enchilada sauce
- 2 bundles green onions
- 1 bag Mexican blended cheese
- 1 tablespoon seasoning salt
- 1 tablespoon pepper
- 1 tablespoon onion powder
- 3.5 lbs carne asada meat diced
- 3 lobsters - 1 for the top, 2 for inside

SEAFOOD GUMBO

Large dice your trinity. Put that to the side.

Dice your sausage, cube your chicken breasts or boneless skinless thigh meat. We like a mixture of half chicken breast and half skinless thigh meat. Clean your shrimp. The crawfish tail meat already comes cleaned and cooked.

Take your cast iron pan, your cup of oil and your cup of flour and heat the pan up. Add the oil, heat that up. Gradually add the flour to make a roux. You have to sit there and stir for about 1.5 to 2 hours until you get a dark-colored roux without burning it. You gotta stay on it! You can't leave the roux. You can't let the roux burn, so you gotta constantly be stirring until it's brown. Make sure it's not sticking to the bottom of the pot. THIS IS THE KEY TO YOUR GUMBO! I repeat, the key to your gumbo is your roux! Do not scorch or burn that! You have to cook it. If you have to take the pan on and off the fire just to control the temperature, then that's what I suggest you do. This is serious.

Take your trinity, your diced chicken and diced sausage in a pot, sauté it in some oil until it starts to turn clear and turns soft. Add the pepper sauce in to taste along with the other seasonings. Keep tasting throughout and adding seasoning throughout. Then you add the chicken broth and bring it to a boil. Once it boils, you take the roux that you'd set to the side fully cooked, and you add it to the pot. Keep stirring until it thickens. It's gonna get thick. Let that boil up for an hour. Then you take your shrimp, crab legs and party wings and add them in and cook them for another hour. You can fry your party wings beforehand, but we prefer to cook them raw.

Add the gumbo filé at the end to taste. The max cook time for a good gumbo with a nice, dark, rich roux is like 2.5 to 3 hours, but you can leave it on as long as you want. WE DON'T PUT OKRA IN OURS!

SEAFOOD GUMBO

- 1 cup of oil
- 1 cup of flour
- 2 cloves garlic
- 4 whole dry bay leaves
- Old bay seasoning
- 1lb Hillshire Farms green label chicken sausage smoked on a rope
  (if you don't eat pork) or andouille sausage
- 2 lbs party wings (depends on who's coming to the party)
- 1lb crawfish tail meat
- 2 green bell peppers
- 1 stalk of celery
- 1 onion (The peppers, celery and onions together is known as the Trinity!)
- 3 lbs snow crab
- 3 lbs king crabs
- Season salt
- Onion powder
- Cajun seasoning (we use Louisiana brand)
- 3 tablespoons pepper sauce
- 4 lbs large shrimp - raw peeled and deveined
- Chicken breast OR boneless skinless thigh meat
  (2.5 lbs if one, or 1.25 lbs of each if you're combining)
- Gumbo filé seasoning
- Cast iron pan
- 1 tablespoon cayenne pepper
- 1 cup flour
- 3 quarts of chicken broth
- 2 cups of water
- Soup kitchen pot (This shit should be the biggest pot that can hold all the shit
  you want to put in there. Ain't no telling how many people you feeding!)

SHRIMP & BOWS

(Shrimp Mac Attack)

Follow the instructions from the Trap Mac, but don't put it in the oven just yet.

Cut half a pound of shrimp into threes and sauté them into your pan with some old bay, some pepper and Cajun seasoning, and add them to your mix. You won't have to worry about whether the raw shrimp is getting cooked fully or not while you're cooking the macaroni mix. Top it with raw shrimp, then bake on 425 degrees until the edges start browning and crusting.

SHRIMP & BOWS

- 1 lb raw shrimp - peeled and deveined
- Old bay seasoning
- Cajun seasoning
- Pepper
- 1 box of small macaroni noodles
- ½ lb sharp cheddar cheese
- ½ lb Kobe jack cheddar cheese
- ½ lb Monterey jack cheese
- ½ lb Mild cheddar cheese
- 2 cans Campbell's cheddar cheese soup
- 2 cans Campbell's roasted garlic mushroom soup
- 1 can Carnation evaporated milk
- ½ cup Kraft cheese whiz in a jar
- Dried parsley flakes
- Seasoning salt
- ½ stick of butter
- 2 dollops sour cream

CHEESE UP LOBSTER MAC

Follow the Trap Mac recipe.

Gut the lobster, clean them, dice the tails. Two get sautéed with old bay seasoning, two go on top raw for the topping. Bake on 425 degrees until the edges start browning and crusting.

CHEESE UP LOBSTER MAC

- 4 lobster tails
- Old bay seasoning
- Everything else from the Trap Mac

IF YOU LIKE SHRIMP & GRITS AND ALL THAT PIMP SH...

Follow the grits instructions of whatever grits you using.

Peel, clean and butterfly your shrimp. Sear them on each side and cook them until they're pink and opaque, while adding seasoning to taste. Strain them and put them to the side.

Put the grits into a bowl and garnish with about 5 shrimps to each bowl. Top with cheese, melted butter and chives.

IF YOU LIKE SHRIMP & GRITS AND ALL THAT PIMP SH...

- 1lb large prawns
- 1 bundle of chives
- HELLA butter (You want to add butter into the grits so it can have that butter taste!)
- Cajun seasoning
- Salt
- 1 cup shredded cheddar cheese
- Old bay
- 1 teaspoon of lemon juice (You can't taste it; this is to cut the saltiness. You'd be like, "God damn! This shit is salty!")
- 1 box of grits

THE BUSS' DOWN
(King Crab Jambalaya Pasta)

This is a lot of shit, and that's why we don't cook it that much. This is original shit, too! Don't get that twisted.

Dice up all your vegetables, sausage and chicken and butterfly, clean, peel and devein your shrimp. Coat your pot with vegetable oil, and sauté your trinity, sausage, shrimp, minced garlic and brown your chicken. Throw your bay leaf in and all the seasonings at once while you're sautéeing it. You want to season it while you're sautéeing it - this is key! Do it to your liking, and you can add pepper sauce here it if you want. Then dump puree and crushed tomatoes in and cook for 15 minutes to get rid of the tomato taste. You want to add Worcestershire sauce once you've cooked in the tomato puree. Add the shrimp in during your last 15 minutes too. Then add your chicken broth. Bring to a boil and then let it reduce. Let it cook down uncovered and the water will start evaporating and get lower.

Cook the pasta al dente - shock them in an ice bath. Put water and ice in your strainer after you drain them, because it preserves them so it doesn't get mushy. This is called blanching them, but we spelled it out for y'all because you may have had to Google that and we know you don't have the time for that. Put the pasta to the side.

Coat a pot with vegetable oil, throw the pasta in, ladle in some of your jambalaya mix and toss it.

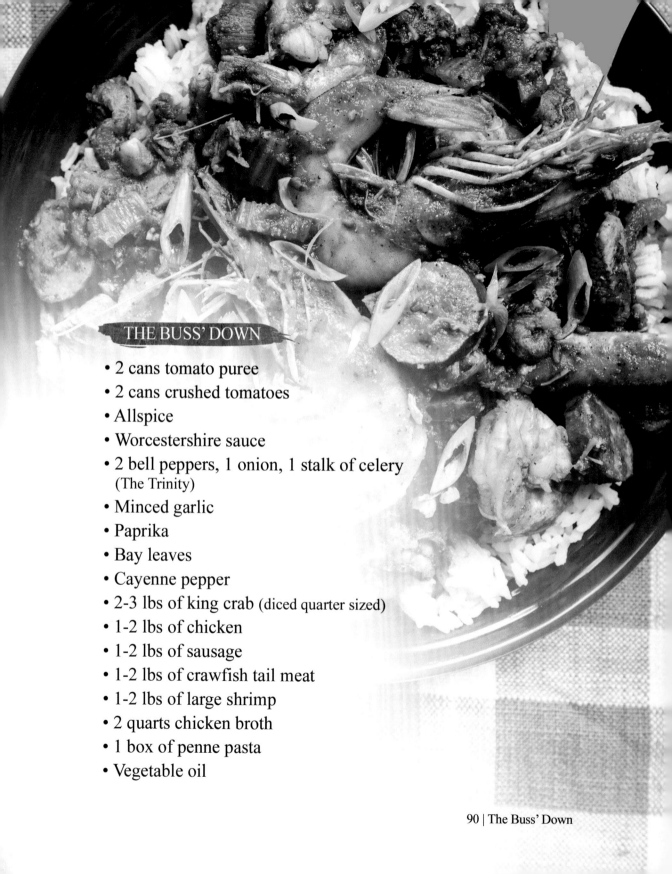

THE BUSS' DOWN

- 2 cans tomato puree
- 2 cans crushed tomatoes
- Allspice
- Worcestershire sauce
- 2 bell peppers, 1 onion, 1 stalk of celery (The Trinity)
- Minced garlic
- Paprika
- Bay leaves
- Cayenne pepper
- 2-3 lbs of king crab (diced quarter sized)
- 1-2 lbs of chicken
- 1-2 lbs of sausage
- 1-2 lbs of crawfish tail meat
- 1-2 lbs of large shrimp
- 2 quarts chicken broth
- 1 box of penne pasta
- Vegetable oil

ALL IN MY GRILL SALMON
(Grilled Salmon)

With the skin on, fillet the salmon. We already told y'all what kind of salmon to get, but we gon' stress it one more time - no foreign-raised salmon!

Take the Cajun blackened seasoning, butter, old bay and garlic powder, and drizzle the melted butter over the fish, adding the seasoning.

Heat up your griddle really hot with some vegetable oil. Place the fish face down, skin side up, and sear it. It's going to get black immediately. Take a fish spatula and flip it, add water to steam and cover it for 15 minutes. Easy!

ALL IN MY GRILL SALMON

- Wild caught socceye Alaskan salmon
  (Nah, that's not a typo, cuz!)
- Cajun blackened seasoning
- Cast iron griddle
- 2 tablespoons of butter
- 2 tablespoons Old Bay
- 2 tablespoons garlic powder
- Vegetable oil

PORK

Cooking on the grill is my favorite thing to do. I grew up barbecuing, and watching my uncles barbecuing. Every family cookout, any repast (which unfortunately there were a lot), weddings, whatever – my uncles would be on the grill. I know some of y'all may not like pork on your fork, so this section won't be for you. But for those of y'all that are with the shits, dig in!

LIVE AT THE BBQ RIBS

Make a seasoning blend to taste. Put it in and stir until it's one color. Take the mustard and lightly rub your ribs down first. Then you take your dry rub and mix it on top of the mustard. Make sure your ribs are dried off at room temperature for the best results. Take a baking sheet or pan, place them down with the bone sticking up and bake them at 375 degrees for 15 minutes. Get them started in the oven and start on your other sides. Once they turn light brown, take them out. We face them down so they don't lose their juices. You want to cook them in their own juices because you can't dry it out.

You should have your grill going now. Take them out of the oven and place them face down so you can seer them in that good juice. Flip them over, smoke them, grill them over mesquite charcoal for about an hour until the bone starts sticking out or you can pull out the bone. Make sure they don't go over 400 degrees and keep some water on your hand. Don't burn your shit because we can't help you then. As you're grilling, pour the Coca-Cola over it gradually.

Take them off, cut them up, place them back in the oven covered with a little bit of water to steam for another 20 minutes at 425 degrees. You can eat them with barbecue sauce on the side but we guarantee you don't need sauce.

LIVE AT THE BBQ RIBS

- 2 racks of baby back ribs
- Mustard
- 1 tablespoon seasoning salt
- 1 tablespoon garlic salt
- 1 tablespoon brown sugar
- 1 tablespoon onion powder
- 1 tablespoon garlic powder
- 1 tablespoon pepper
- 1 tablespoon smoked paprika
- 1 cup Coca-Cola
- Mesquite charcoal for the grill
- Your choice of BBQ sauce (optional)

YOUNG CHOPS ON THE HEAT
(Pork Chops)

Coat the tenderloins in olive oil and add your seasonings. Take some tongs and sear the fat off the tenderloins first, then sear it on all sides.

Take the griddle and place it in the oven on 375, and cook for about 45 minutes. Let rest upon taking out.

YOUNG CHOPS ON THE HEAT

- Kosher salt
- Coarse pepper
- Smoked paprika
- Onion powder
- Olive oil
- Pork tenderloins - thick cut
- Cast iron griddle

ABOUT THE AUTHORS

TRAP KITCHEN

Chefs Malachi "Spanky" Jenkins and Roberto "News" Smith are members of the historically feuding gangs, the Bloods and the Crips. Introduced by a mutual friend, their love of food became their passport into the culinary world and the beginning of a long and prosperous relationship. Having been featured in *Ebony Magazine, Huffington Post, The Today Show, Fox News, Crime Story Daily* and *Martha and Snoop's Potluck Party*, they are now media darlings, taking the world by storm.

MARISA MENDEZ

Marisa Mendez is a media personality and journalist who has built her reputation around all things digital, working for some of the biggest names in entertainment and hip-hop. The New Jersey native is most recognized for her work launching Funk Flex's In Flex We Trust blog, as a cast member on Hot 97's Ebro In The Morning and as a host for Diddy's television network, REVOLT TV. She is also a digital strategist, and has managed social media campaigns for Pusha T's clothing line Play Cloths, French Montana, Swizz Beatz and more.

TRAP KITCHEN

BANGIN' RECIPES FROM COMPTON

TRAP KITCHEN DEDICATION

Thank you for judging us by our talent and not our appearance, and never letting our backgrounds or our past get in the way of our future.

ROBERTO "NEWS" SMITH

I never imagined cooking would take me this far in my career. I dedicate this cook book to the future generations to come, and I hope it inspires everyone reading this to follow your dreams and put action behind your dreams. Sabra Jenkins, my Mother, for all of her love and support.

MALACHI "SPANKY" JENKINS

Thank you first and foremost to Kathy Iandoli - this opportunity wouldn't have happened without you! You are the GOAT! Thank you to Marvis for trusting me with this project, as well as Spank and News. Of course, have to shout out mom and dad for encouraging the writer in me since a young buck! Thank you to Jay for holding down the tapes, Jamal for your endless creativity, and to Carol, Zombz, Tori, Kiana and Chels for no real reason other than it feeling wrong to have thank you's and not say your names, LOL! Most importantly, though - thank you to the man upstairs. God is good! This is dedicated to my baby angel Parker; we miss you every day. #PowerOfParker

MARISA MENDEZ

TRAP KITCHEN CREDITS

Photo Shoot Locations
Kitchen NYC
Egg Studio NYC

Food Photographer: Teddy Wolff
Food Stylist: Martha Tinkler
Trap Kitchen Photographer: Audrey Melton
Creative Direction: Joshua Wirth

Creative Consultants:
Roberta Magrini
Kathy Iandoli
Nisa Ahmad

Editor in Chief: Marvis Johnson

Also Available From
VODKA&MILK

The Purple Don
Solomon

Revelations:
The New Scriptures
Solomon

They:
Want You Dead
Solomon

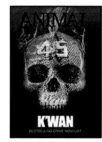

Animal 4.5
K'wan
Write 2 Eat Concepts

Captain Save-A-Hoe
iiKane

Cham-Pain
iiKane

Commissary Kitchen:
My Infamous Prison Cookbook
Albert "Prodigy" Johnson
w/ Kathy Iandoli

The Infamous
Solomon

Hoodlum 2
The Good Son
K'wan
Write 2 Eat Concepts

**All The Wrong
Places**
G.I.F.T.D

Quantum Assassin
Chainworld
Matt Langley

**A Talent For
Trouble**
MOVIE